Scholastic BookFiles

A READING GUIDE TO

Ella Enchanted

by Gail Carson Levine

Irene Connelly

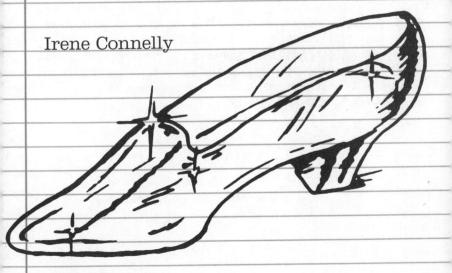

SCHOLASTIC
REFERENCE

Copyright © 2004 by Scholastic Inc.
Interview © 2004 by Gail Carson Levine
Trifle Recipe © 2004 by Kristin James

All rights reserved. Published by Scholastic Inc.

SCHOLASTIC, SCHOLASTIC REFERENCE, SCHOLASTIC BOOKFILES, and associated logos are trademarks and/or registered trademarks of Scholastic Inc.

No part of this publication may be reproduced, or stored in a retrieval system, or transmitted in any form or by any means, electronic, mechanical, photocopying, recording, or otherwise, without written permission of the publisher. For information regarding permission, write to Scholastic Inc., Attention: Permissions Department, 557 Broadway, New York, NY 10012.

0-439-53823-8

10 9 8 7 6 5 4 3 2 1   04 05 06 07 08

Composition by Brad Walrod/High Text Graphics, Inc.
Cover and interior design by Red Herring Design

Printed in the U.S.A.   23
First printing, June 2004

Contents

"My dad was a businessman who ran a commercial art studio and loved to write. My mom was a teacher who would write full-length verse plays for her students to perform. They both loved creativity and creative people. And that reverence was passed on to me and my older sister..."

—Gail Carson Levine, interview,
Authors & Artists for Young Adults

Born on September 17, 1947, in New York City, Gail Carson was raised in the borough of Manhattan. She remembers it as a great place to grow up because in those days city kids could be independent at a young age. They didn't depend on their parents to drive them places. "By the sixth grade I was allowed to go on the subway alone," Gail has said. She and her friends happily explored by train and on foot. "New York City was our oyster," she has said.

Through their own lives, Gail's parents demonstrated the importance of the arts to their children. The impression was lasting: Gail became a writer, and her older sister, Rani, became a painter.

Gail began writing at a young age. She was president of a writing club called the Scribble Scrabble Club in elementary school, and in high school she published some poetry. At the time, however, she had no plans to be a writer. Instead, she wanted to be an actress, or a painter like her older sister.

As a high school student, Gail had a leading role in *Androcles and the Lion*, a play by George Bernard Shaw, and she worked in a summer theater program after her junior year. With friends, she started a student theater troupe that performed at hospitals and nursing homes.

In college, Gail majored in philosophy and has said that there was no way she ever thought she would be a professional writer. She continued to act, "and after college I was in a couple of productions with a Brooklyn theater group," she said. "Then I lost interest [in being an actress]." Her interest in painting and drawing, however, survived. In 1967 she married David Levine, and in 1969 she received her B.A. from New York's City College.

From 1970 until *Ella Enchanted* was published in 1997, Gail Carson Levine worked for New York State as an employment interviewer and then as a welfare administrator. She told *Contemporary Authors*, "The earlier experience was more direct and satisfying, and I enjoy thinking that a bunch of people somewhere are doing better today than they might have done if not for me. . . . I haven't yet found a way to write about the subject, but I hope to someday."

While working full-time, she continued to paint and take art classes. She thought of herself as a visual artist, but she has said she judged her own work very harshly: "I was too self-critical, and so the process wasn't pleasant."

Gail Carson Levine's first writing experience as an adult came when she and her husband collaborated on a children's musical called *Spacenapped*. She wrote the story and her husband wrote the music and lyrics for the songs.

The experience of creating *Spacenapped* was one event that brought Gail closer to writing stories. Other things in her life also drew her to writing. Levine meditates, and she has told her publisher, HarperCollins, that "one time when I was meditating, I started thinking, *Gee, Gail, you love stories—you read all the time. How come you never tell yourself a story?"* These thoughts led her to take a children's-book illustration and writing class. "During the class I discovered how much I liked to write—and how little I liked to illustrate." She was now sure of what she wanted to do with her life: write stories. This discovery was like a lightbulb turning on, she has said.

Over the next nine years she wrote a dozen picture books, none of which were published. She continued to take writing classes and joined writers' groups. Gail sent the manuscript for *Ella* (later re-titled *Ella Enchanted*) to an agent she met at a writing conference. This manuscript was published by HarperCollins in 1997 and became a 1998 Newbery Honor book. These events changed Levine's life dramatically. After *Ella Enchanted* came out, she quit her day job and began writing full-time, the dream of many writers!

Since then, Levine has published eleven books: the novels *Dave at Night*, based on her father's experiences growing up in a Jewish orphanage in New York during the 1920s; *The Wish*, about an unpopular eighth-grader; *The Two Princesses of Bamarre*, about a princess on a quest; a picture book, *Betsy Who Cried Wolf*; and The Princess Tales series.

Gail Carson Levine lives with her husband, David, and an Airedale named Baxter in a 200-year-old farmhouse in the Hudson Valley, about an hour north of New York City. Her favorite things to do when she's not writing? "Spend time with my husband and friends, walk the dog, walk around New York City, visit museums, listen to NPR [National Public Radio]." She also runs a writing workshop for kids and travels often, talking to teachers and students about writing and books.

How *Ella Enchanted* Came About

"...When I thought about Cinderella's character, I realized she was too much of a Goody-Two-Shoes for me, and I would hate her before I finished ten pages."

–Gail Carson Levine, in *Contemporary Authors*

Why didn't Cinderella ever stand up for herself? She did as she was told, slaved for her wicked stepmother and stepsisters without rebelling. She never ran away or picked a fight. She just sat around *wishing*. These are the kinds of things Gail Carson Levine was thinking about when she started the writing project that would become *Ella Enchanted*.

Levine was taking a children's-book writing course at The New School in New York and wasn't sure what to write about. She decided to do a Cinderella story because it already had a plot. It also gave her a chance to tackle some of her questions about the story, such as why Cinderella never stood up for herself and told her stepmother, "No." Levine notes that in the fairy tale there is only one task Cinderella has to accomplish on her own behalf— getting home before midnight—"and she blows it." Levine knew she couldn't write about a standard Cinderella. For two weeks, she struggled with the problem. As she says in *Contemporary Authors*: "That's when I came up with the curse: She's only good because she has to be, and she is in constant rebellion." Then Levine was "liberated to write the story."

Ella Enchanted took two years to write. Gail Levine was working full-time, and she spent almost four hours a day commuting to and from her job in Manhattan. Much of the book was written on commuter trains.

Writing *Ella Enchanted* gave Levine a chance to explore the "missing details" in fairy tales that hadn't bothered her as a kid, but perplexed her as an adult. For instance, she had always wondered why the elves abandon the shoemaker in "The Shoemaker and the Elves." "I came up with one answer, but many are possible," she has said.

While writing and exploring, she got "sidetracked," as writers often do. She ended up throwing out hundreds of pages and "going back to about page twenty, where I had left the real story," she told *Authors & Artists for Young Adults*. Once Levine had found her story and completed it, she sent off the manuscript to an agent who could bring it to the attention of editors at different publishing houses. Her life would never be the same!

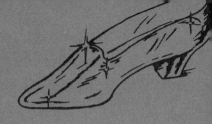

An Interview with Gail Carson Levine

♦ *The fairy Lucinda gave Ella the magic "gift" of obedience. As the human writer, what gifts did you give your heroine?*

I made Ella a heroine—brave, smart, sure of herself, certain of her opinions, and astonishingly good at languages. She's so handicapped by Lucinda's gift that she needs many strengths to offset it.

♦ *Ella's world is full of people and creatures who speak a variety of languages that you've created for them. How did you go about inventing these languages—were they inspired by their speakers? For instance, is there a reason why the biggest creatures, the giants, use so many words to say a simple "hello" in Abdegi?*

Yes, aspects of some of the languages were inspired by the speakers. The giants are such jovial and emotional creatures that their "hellos" would naturally be lengthy. They'd want to make sure that the depth and sincerity of their welcomes are understood. They have lots of emotive sounds in their language, and their alphabet is only vowels and percussive [sharp, striking] consonants. Abdegi, the name of the language, is also the first six letters in its alphabet. Ogrese is sneaky and insinuating, just like the ogres. I wanted the languages to look different, so the double letters in Ogrese are capitalized. Gnomic has a lot of guttural sounds, and it's punctuated and capitalized backwards, with the punctuation at the beginning of the sentence and the capital letter at the end of the word. Elfian is phonetically like English, only nonsense words. I was thinking of Italian when I invented Ayorthaian, and so every word begins with a vowel and ends with the same vowel. I kept a glossary of the words, but I didn't do much with grammar. If you look closely you'll find that plurals and tenses are haphazard.

◆ *Was reading a big part of your childhood? What were some of your favorite books?*

I was a monster reader as a kid. I loved Louisa May Alcott's books and L. M. Montgomery's. I loved *Peter Pan* and *Heidi* and *Bambi* and *Black Beauty.* When I was a little older I loved *Jane Eyre* and *Pride and Prejudice.*

◆ *You have said that for you, writing is a happy process. Can you explain why? What is an average writing day like for you?*

Well, it's not always so happy. I've recently started a new novel, and I couldn't get the voice [how the narrator/character thinks and speaks] right. I think I've got it now, but till I did I was pretty miserable. When the writing isn't going well, I'm not happy. What I mean when I say it's a happy process is that I'm not too hard on myself when I write. My criticisms of my work tend to be specific and useful. Like I know when a bit of dialogue isn't right, and I know how to approach making it better.

When I surprise myself or write something funny or pull something off that I wasn't sure I could do, then I'm elated. Still, I'm a bit uneasy till I've written a whole first draft. Then I'm deliriously happy, and I love to revise. All I have to do then is to make things better—it's heaven.

I've been traveling so much lately that a typical day has started with leaving for the airport, writing while I wait for departure, and writing during the flight. When I'm home for a while and I haven't got a complete first draft, I'll write for a couple of hours and then deal with the other side of a writer's life—answering e-mails, looking at contracts, answering fan mail, etc. When I've got a complete draft, I can revise endlessly and the hours fly by.

I do other things, too, of course. Every day I take the dog for a long walk, meditate, spend time with my husband.

◆ *Ella spends much of her time learning to deal with creatures different from herself, and she seems to value what they have to teach her. Do your dogs inspire any parts of your work?*

We only have one dog, thank heaven (considering the dog we have). Baxter's a one-and-a-half-year-old totally mischievous Airedale who eats anything that crosses his path, including socks, a pen, and two pairs of eyeglasses. One pair was the bifocals of a very elderly friend. [Baxter] hasn't made it into one of my books yet, but maybe he will.

A dog is an important character in [my book] *The Wish*, however. Reggie is based on our first Airedale, Archie, and the incident in

The Wish when Reggie pees at a very bad moment in a very inappropriate place comes from life! My husband, David, and I went for dinner to the home of new friends, and Archie was invited because they also had a young Airedale. Soon after we arrived, Archie peed on the leg of our new friends' claw-footed antique dining-room table.

♦ *You regularly run a writing workshop for kids. What kinds of things have you learned from this workshop, and have they had an effect on your own writing?*

I've developed lots of exercises for the kids, and because of the experience of teaching them, I've written a book for kids about writing. I always do the exercises with the kids, and I've discovered that if an exercise works for me it works for them, and if it doesn't work for them it doesn't work for me, either. I don't mean that the kids write at an adult level. They don't, but it seems that writing is writing, no matter how old you are.

The kids are game for anything, and school has taught them to be able to perform at the drop of a hat. When I give out an exercise, they start right in on it. They don't agonize and tear their hair. I'm always impressed by that, and when I'm with them I write more spontaneously than I do in my office at home. And even at home I may be better at plunging right in than I would be without the experience of working with the kids.

Last year I gave them this story starter: *Erica goes to sleep over at her friend Josie's house. When Erica gets there, Josie takes out her collection of shrunken animal heads.* I started to work on it along with the kids. Shortly thereafter I was invited to submit a short story for an anthology [a published collection] of mysterious stories, and that story starter was the genesis [beginning] of the story I submitted, which was accepted by the editor.

But mainly I love being with the kids, watching them grow and become better writers. I'm also often surprised and delighted by the stuff they come up with. The workshop is the best part of my week.

◆ *Do you think that working with a group and getting feedback from different people is helpful to a writer? Do you share your work in progress with anyone, or are you private about it?*

For me, feedback is essential. I learned to write by taking classes, joining critique groups, and acting on almost all the criticism that came my way. For years I took the same class over and over at the New School in New York City because it was so helpful. The teacher tended to concentrate on making the story exciting, keeping readers worrying and turning pages, which I think is the number one issue in writing for kids. I hope I've internalized this by now. These days I have only one critique buddy, the marvelous young-adult writer Joan Abelove. And of course I depend very much on the criticism of my wonderful editor at HarperCollins, Alix Reid.

However, there are some caveats. I don't show my work right away to Alix. I wait till I'm pretty satisfied with it. The reason is that her criticism carries extra weight because she's my editor, and I don't want to hear from her while I'm still exploring my story. Joan is perfect because she's a peer. I take her criticism very seriously, but I can evaluate it objectively and ignore it when it doesn't seem right for me.

◆ *Most of your books use elements of traditional fairy tales. What is it about fairy tales that attracts you as a writer, and why do you think we as readers return again and again to these stories?*

I'm attracted to fairy tales for lots of reasons. The first, and the reason the stories survive, is that they're about important stuff. For example, "Cinderella" is about being unappreciated, and I think we all feel that way fairly regularly. Or, "Hansel and Gretel" is about abandonment. And most are about love in one way or another.

They're also full of action and drama. A lot is at stake and there's never a dull moment, which is wonderful for a kids'-book writer.

The breakneck pace often covers grave [serious] gaps in logic. Fairy tales are often supremely goofy. For example, "The Princess and the Pea" presents a completely nutty way to find a future ruler. Or take love at first sight—in "Sleeping Beauty" the prince falls in love with the princess while she's still asleep. They haven't said a single word to each other! All he knows about her is that she's pretty and doesn't snore! In "Snow White," the prince falls in love with a maiden he thinks is dead! This wacky stuff is enormous fun to work with. What's more, one of my missions is to put the kibosh on [put a stop to] beauty as a sufficient reason for love—in my versions there has to be more to it than that.

Another reason is the rich detail: cloaks of invisibility, jewels or snakes and insects coming out of a maiden's mouth, purses that fill themselves, tablecloths that deliver food endlessly, princes turned into toads, seven-league boots. In fairy tales this super stuff flies by. You don a cloak of invisibility and—*poof!*—you're invisible. But what does that feel like? What does it feel like to turn into a toad or a deer or a stone statue? I love to slow down the fairy tales and help the reader experience these extraordinary events.

Is there a piece of advice you like to give to beginning writers?

My success has come as a huge surprise to me. I wish someone had said to me that *anything* can happen, and that I should take risks. There's more to lose by being overly cautious than by taking a few chances.

My advice is to keep writing! Writing is deceptively hard, unlike learning a musical instrument, which is obviously hard. With writing, you know how to read, you know how to recognize a good story, you know how to form words and sentences. Writing a story should be a snap. But it's not. It takes a lot of practice, but you'll get better. You may abandon most of your stories before you finish them. But if you keep writing, you'll still get better. You may hate the stuff you write. But if you keep writing, you'll get better.

Chapter 1

- "Instead of making me docile, Lucinda's curse made a rebel of me," says Ella. What kinds of problems does Ella's "curse" create for her, and how do you see her fight back?

Chapter 2

- What do Sir Peter's words and actions reveal about the kind of person he is?
- How is Prince Charmont's attitude different from that of everyone else at the funeral? Is he the kind of person you'd want to be around if you were going through a hard time?

Chapter 3

- What roles do Hattie and Olive play in Ella's story? Do the girls seem familiar?
- Why do you think Ella's mother never told her who her fairy godmother is?

Chapter 4

- Mandy refuses to do "big magic" and sticks to "small magic that can't hurt anybody." Does it make sense that the ability to do magic comes with so much responsibility? Do you think that every talent or gift comes with responsibilities?

- Sir Peter describes Ella as "strong" and "determined." How does she demonstrate these qualities when dealing with her father?

Chapter 5
- How do you feel about Sir Peter? What kind of father is he?

Chapter 6
- Do you think Ella's talent for mimicry could be useful? How might it help her?

Chapter 7
- If you knew someone could tell you what the future holds for you, would you want to know? Do you think the gnome's warning will help Ella?

Chapter 8
- How are Hattie and Olive different from each other?
- How would you stand up to Hattie if you were in Ella's place?

Chapter 9
- In what ways does Ella *not* fit in at school?
- Why do you think Areida wants to be friends with Ella?

Chapter 10
- What subjects come easiest to Ella? Why do you think this is the case?

Chapter 11

- Ella returns to her "old game" in order to cope with her teachers' orders. What is the "game"?
- Do you think it was right for Ella to give Hattie the bogwort? Do you think it was worth it?

Chapter 12

- Hattie orders Ella to end her friendship with Areida—how does that order, along with the letters Ella reads in her magic book, affect her? What would you do in Ella's place?

Chapter 13

- What does it mean when the elf woman looks into Ella's eyes and pronounces her "not like [her] father"?
- When Slannen shows Agulen's pottery to Ella, why does the figure of the wolf attract her so?

Chapter 14

- The ogres figure out how obedient Ella is . . . yet *she* ends up giving the orders. How does she pull this off?

Chapter 15

- What skills does Ella use to "tame" the ogres?

Chapter 16

- What do both the content and the spelling of Hattie's and Olive's letters tell you about the girls?

Chapter 17

- Lucinda gives the newlywed giants a "gift." Could this gift turn into a big problem? Why do you think so?

Chapter 18

- Lucinda orders Ella: "Be happy to be blessed with such a lovely quality." Why does Ella suddenly feel "free" for the first time since her mother's death? Is this a good thing?
- How do you think Ella's situation would be different if her father knew about the curse?

Chapter 19

- Mandy advises Ella not to be happy about being obedient. "Be whatever you feel about it," she says. Do you think this a good command?
- Does Ella still have feelings for Char, even though magic causes her to be "enamored of" Sir Edmund? Do you think emotions can be genuine if they're caused by magic?

Chapter 20

- What do you think of Lucinda's gift to Sir Peter and Dame Olga? Can you imagine some of its possible consequences?

Chapter 21

- What kinds of things happen to Char and Ella during their time together at the wedding? Does something shift in their relationship?

Chapter 22

- How might Sir Peter's confession to Dame Olga that he's broke end up affecting Ella?
- Why does Hattie prevent Ella from seeing Char?

Chapter 23

- If Dame Olga loves Ella's father so much, why do she and her daughters treat Ella so badly? What might she hope to gain?
- Why does Ella believe her father is the only person who can help her? If you were Ella, would you ask Sir Peter for help?

Chapter 24

- How does Ella and Char's relationship develop through their correspondence? What sorts of things do they learn about each other?

Chapter 25

- Do you think Ella's decision to give up Char is the right one? Do you agree with her reasoning or not?

Chapter 26

- What do you think of Lucinda's attempt to help Ella without breaking her vow not to do "big magic"? Does it explain the familiar fairy-tale elements in this chapter?

Chapter 27

- Is Ella "a fool" for behaving so much like herself? Is it surprising that Char doesn't recognize her?

Chapter 28

- Why do you think Char has decided never to marry?

Chapter 29

- Mandy says, "Nothing is small magic in a moment like this." What does she mean?
- How does Ella break the curse once and for all? What is it that gives her the power?
- Ella proposes to Char—why is this significant?

Epilogue

- What do you think of Lucinda's wedding gift?
- Why does Ella refuse to become a princess but take the titles of Court Linguist and Cook's Helper?

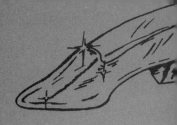

"I had a fairy godmother, and Mother asked her to take the curse away. But my fairy godmother said Lucinda was the only one who could remove it. However, she also said it might be broken someday without Lucinda's help."

—Ella, *Ella Enchanted*

Ella Enchanted is the story of Ella of Frell, a girl cursed at birth when a misguided fairy gives her a terrible "gift." She goes on a quest to persuade the fairy to remove the curse, but ultimately it is her own strength that saves her.

The fairy Lucinda means to give Ella a gift when she says to the crying infant, "My gift is obedience. Ella will always be obedient." Lucinda doesn't foresee the terrible consequences of this gift, but Ella must live with them. "Anyone could control me with an order," she tells us. "If you commanded me to cut off my own head, I'd have to do it."

When Ella's mother dies, her father, Sir Peter, decides to send her to finishing school with Hattie and Olive, the spoiled, stupid daughters of Dame Olga. She leaves behind her new friend, Prince

Charmont of Frell. Her beloved Mandy, the cook, gives her the gift of a magic book and reveals that *she* is Ella's fairy godmother.

Hattie is a "monster" who discovers that Ella must always obey an order, and makes her life at school miserable by turning her into a servant. When Hattie orders her to stop seeing her only school friend, Areida, Ella turns to her magic book. In it, she reads of her father's plans to attend a wedding of giants at which fairies are likely to be present. Ella decides to run away from school to go to the wedding. If Lucinda is there, perhaps she will break the curse.

Pursuing Lucinda at the wedding, Ella discovers that the fairy is famous for giving misguided gifts. Lucinda doesn't understand why Ella would want to give back her "gift" and orders her to be happy with it. Ella obeys Lucinda's command and her feelings change entirely. "The curse [has] turned into a blessing," Ella tells the reader. She believes she can embrace whatever happens.

After Sir Peter fails to marry Ella to a rich man, he decides to marry Dame Olga for her money. At the wedding, Ella meets up with Char. They skip the wedding ball and go exploring. In a tower room, they find an unusual pair of slippers made of glass. Ella tries them on and they fit her exactly.

After the wedding, Sir Peter confesses to Dame Olga that he is a poor man. Despite her horror at this news, she loves him— thanks to the fairy's gift—but she doesn't feel the same way about Ella. Sir Peter tells his wife that Ella must not be treated like a servant in her own home and, though Dame Olga agrees with him, she looks at Ella with "pure venom."

Ella begins to feel the consequences of her father's deception of Dame Olga. Hattie orders her new stepsister around just as she did at school. When Char comes to visit, Ella is ordered to stay in her room. She won't be able to see him before he leaves for a year in the royal court at Ayortha. So she writes him a letter, and the two friends begin a long correspondence.

Sir Peter resumes his travels, and Dame Olga moves Ella's things to the servants' quarters. Hattie reveals to everyone that, for some reason, Ella "does whatever she is told." From now on, Ella will be a servant, says Dame Olga. The only power Ella has is her quick wit, and her only comfort is her correspondence with Char. Their letters are frequent and grow more affectionate. Finally, Char confesses his love for her. As she reads the letter, Ella realizes she loves him, too.

But can she marry him? Ella realizes that she "wouldn't escape the curse by marrying Char." In fact, Char and his kingdom could be harmed if her obedience were to be discovered by an enemy. As long as she lives under the fairy's curse, Ella can't marry her true love. Miserable, she tries to make him hate her by writing a fake letter from Hattie.

Meanwhile, Mandy has shown Lucinda how all her thoughtless "gifts" have harmed people. Lucinda vows to do no more "big magic," so she cannot break the curse she put on Ella so many years before.

Three balls are being held to celebrate Char's return from his year in Ayortha. Everyone believes he will choose his bride during the festivities. In secret, Mandy and Lucinda make sure Ella attends the festivities. Ella wears a mask and disguises her voice to keep Charmont from recognizing her, and they dance together each night. When a jealous Hattie pulls off her mask, Ella's identity is revealed. She escapes, losing one of her glass slippers.

Char arrives at Olga's house looking for the girl whose slipper he's found. Hattie and Olive try on the shoe, and it doesn't fit. It fits Ella, of course. "Marry me!" Char says. It is an order, so she agrees, hoping someone will order her not to. In those moments, she realizes that she must refuse him in order to save them both. After a terrible struggle, she is able to say no. The curse is broken because Ella finally has both reason and strength enough to break it. She no longer poses a threat to Char's and Kyrria's safety. Ella also knows she loves Char enough to marry him of her own free will, so she goes down on one knee and proposes to him.

And they live happily ever after!

Thinking about the plot

- Why is the fairy's well-intentioned gift really a curse?
- How is Ella's story like the familiar Cinderella story? In what ways is it different?
- Magic plays a big part in the story. Does it help solve problems or help create them? Why do you think so?
- What are Ella's greatest strengths and how does she demonstrate them?

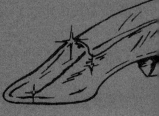

"My first landmark would be the elves' Forest. After the Forest I would come to another fork. The road to the left, which I was not to take, led to the Fens, where the ogres lived. The road on the right would take me to the giants. When the cows became as big as barns, I would be there."

—Ella, *Ella Enchanted*

The kingdom of Kyrria, where Ella's story takes place, exists in a world of its own. Ruled by King Jerrold, the kingdom is home to humans, fairies, ogres, gnomes, giants, and many other creatures. Kyrria is not unlike the medieval settings of many familiar fairy tales: There are castles, quests, and traveling knights, as well as a titled class supported by traders and merchants like Ella's father. There are tapestries and dragons. But in this country, the dragons are real.

We learn very soon that Ella lives in a place where people have fairy godmothers, centaurs snack on apples, and elves make pottery. This is the reality of the story, and we believe in Ella's world from the beginning—*of course* she has a fairy godmother! *Of course* there are centaurs and a dragon in the royal menagerie!

Ella lives in Frell, an important town in Kyrria. She grows up in her father's manor house. The family is well-to-do because Sir Peter is a successful trader. Their household staff includes a cook (Mandy), maids, and other servants. The house has "forty-two windows and a fireplace in every room," according to Hattie.

The throw rug that used to lie under Lady Eleanor's chair in the great hall features a scene of a hound and hunters chasing a boar. There is nothing remarkable about it until the day of Lady Eleanor's funeral, when the rug comes alive for Ella. She feels the movements and emotions of characters in the scene, and she feels as if she's been "in the rug." Mandy tells her that it is a silly rug, a fairy joke. In Ella's world, magic is an everyday thing.

A long walk from Ella's home takes her to the old castle, which is said to be haunted. Abandoned when King Jerrold was a boy, the castle is reopened "on special occasions, for private balls, weddings, and the like." The castle's overgrown gardens feature a grove of candle trees, "small trees that had been pruned and tied to wires to make them grow in the shape of candelabra." Ella goes here to make a wish because she wants to "make it in the place where it would have the best chance of being granted."

The new castle, where Prince Charmont and his parents live, is nearby. Ella and Char's second meeting takes place in the royal menagerie, just outside the palace walls. It is one of the places Ella loves best, and she wants to say good-bye to it before she leaves for school. Except for the hydra and the baby dragon, the exotic animals—"the unicorn, the herd of centaurs, and the gryphon family"—live on an island surrounded by an extension of the castle moat.

Ella attends a finishing school in the town of Jenn, reached after a long trip south of Frell. Except for the enormous ornamental shrubs (pruned to look like "wide-skirted maidens") outside it, the school is an ordinary wooden house. Her "lavender cloud" of a bedroom and the topiary seem to be the only things about her school's physical environment that impress Ella.

Since the story is told from Ella's point of view, we only know what she tells us. Her time at school is so unpleasant that she doesn't pay much attention to her surroundings—she just tries to survive. Similarly, during the time when she slaves for "Mum Olga," her focus is on getting through the days, and not on her surroundings. We learn little about the house where she lives with her stepmother and stepsisters.

When Ella heads off to find Lucinda, her travels take her through the part of Kyrria where the giants live. She knows she'll be getting close when the cows become as big as barns. Human guests at the giants' wedding struggle with knives and forks the size of axes and shovels. The size of the giants and their things gives us an idea of what it's like to be Ella in their midst.

The kingdom closest to Kyrria is Ayortha, home of Ella's school friend, Areida. Char spends a year in Ayortha as a guest of the royal court on a sort of royal exchange program. Ayorthaians are known for their wonderful singing and for their unusual attitude toward speech. From Char's letters to Ella, we learn that the kind and smiling Ayorthaians "think before they speak, and often conclude . . . that nothing need be said." The ordinary Ayorthaians are talkative, but the nobles at court are not, usually uttering a single word at a time, or maybe a phrase. "Once a week they utter a complete sentence. On their birthdays they grant the world an entire paragraph," Char writes in a letter to Ella.

In this world, as in our own, there is a variety of languages spoken by different people (and nonhumans). As Ella encounters different people and beings, she learns their languages: Gnomic, Ayorthaian, Ogrese, Elfian, Abdegi, and more. Languages can reveal much about the cultures of those who speak them. We can also learn about characters through the *way* they use their language. The author has written a story that is rich not only in characters, but also in its cultures, creating a complete, believable world.

Thinking about the setting

- Does Ella's world, which is so different from our own, feel real to you?
- Do the different characters and their languages contribute to your impression of the world around Ella?
- Do we learn things about the narrator based on the way she describes the setting?

> "I was made anew. Ella. Just Ella. Not Ella, the slave. Not a scullery maid. Not Lela. Not Eleanor. Ella. Myself unto myself. One. Me."

—Ella, *Ella Enchanted*

A story's theme is its main idea. It is an author's general statement (or statements) about life. Four important themes in Ella's story are being your own person, the power of words, humor, and love.

Being your own person: independence versus obedience

Ella isn't the only one who suffers from the curse of obedience. Many of us feel as though we're under a kind of curse—one that makes us feel obligated to meet everybody's expectations, to be the person others want us to be. There is a struggle between the parts of us that are obedient and the parts of us that need to be independent, to be who *we* want to be.

Because of the fairy's curse, Ella is a person who must constantly fight with herself. She is also "in danger at every moment"; vulnerable to the commands of others. "If you commanded me to cut off my own head, I'd have to do it," Ella tells the reader. Her need to be independent makes her life even more difficult. If she were less independent and intelligent, the curse of obedience might seem less oppressive to her. However, her independent nature makes her rebel against the curse and find a way to remove it so she can be her own person.

Ella has fought the fairy's "gift" all her life. With those she loves and trusts, Ella turns obedience into a game. Mandy's gentle orders, like "Hold this bowl while I beat the eggs," are met with a playful resistance—Ella will hold the bowl, but walk around with it so that Mandy has to follow her around the kitchen. Although she is being obedient, she is doing it in a way that makes the action her own. Lady Eleanor encourages Ella's attempts to be independent. She seems to understand how hard life is for her daughter.

This game of defiance and obedience is a way for Ella to be her own person, if only for a moment. She can resist direct commands by waiting until the last possible second to obey, but resistance costs her so much "—in breathlessness, nausea, dizziness, and other complaints. . . . Even a few minutes [are] a desperate struggle." Ella feels physical consequences, as well as emotional ones, when she fights against her own will to obey a command.

At school, she retaliates against Hattie's barrage of commands with pranks such as releasing spiders into her bed. These are the only weapons available to Ella in her struggle for independence.

However, they won't work with her teachers. Playing a "tiresome game," she must remind herself constantly to follow their endless orders so she doesn't stand out. The other girls seem to have no trouble obeying the teachers. It is Ella, who has no choice but to obey, who has such difficulty doing it.

Ella becomes a perfect student, but anger continues to build inside her. At night, she imagines what she would do if she were free of the curse. "At dinner I'd paint lines of gravy on my face and hurl meat pasties at Manners Mistress," Ella tells the reader.

Ella's decision to leave school to find Lucinda may be the biggest and most important decision she has ever been able to make for herself. But when she arrives at the giants' wedding, she receives what may be the most dangerous order anyone has ever given her—Lucinda's order to be *happy* about being obedient. "She turned you from half puppet to all puppet," Mandy tells her. Even her father finds Ella's joyful obedience strange, though he tries to benefit from it by arranging a profitable but loveless marriage.

While slaving for her stepfamily, Ella has to cope with something else: Char's love. As long as she is under Lucinda's spell, it is dangerous for Ella to marry Char. If anyone outside her family were to discover her obedience, she could be used as a weapon against Char and the entire kingdom. Ella could be ordered to do anything. Unable to act out of her own free will and be herself, she can't be with the person she loves. She can't live the life she wants.

Char's marriage proposal takes the form of an unintentional order: "Say you'll marry me." This is a threat to Ella, who believes they are all doomed if she says yes. He is "too precious to lose . . . too precious to marry." Their marriage could destroy him. A battle rages inside her. The obedient Ella and the independent, *real* Ella are fighting as never before. Trying to resist speaking, she finds inside herself "room for only one truth: I must save Char."

When she finds the power to refuse Char's command, she finds herself "ready to defy anyone." The spell has been broken without a fairy's magic. Ella feels "larger, fuller, more complete, no longer divided against myself—compulsion to comply against wish to refuse." A "massive burden" has been shed. She is free to be herself and live her life as she chooses.

The power of words

Another theme running through the book is the power of words. This power is expressed in different ways. Ella's gift for languages and her ability to communicate with many kinds of people and creatures is one of her greatest strengths. It saves her life on at least one occasion. Not only can Ella speak Ogrese, for example, but she also figures out how to talk to the ogres using their own tricks. "My voice had been persuasive; might not persuasion have other uses? Could I mimic the ogres? Could I speak with their persuasive power?" By doing so, she saves her own life and the lives of Char and his knights.

For Ella and Char, words are an important way of learning about each other and about the world. They cement their relationship with letters. Their correspondence is rich and full of detail because they are interested in what goes on around them as well as inside them. The two reach out using words, even when they aren't separated.

Words can be used in different ways to achieve power. Hattie, Olive, and Dame Olga use words to make complaints and demands, and also to hurt others. Hattie and Olive, we learn, don't even use words very *well* to do this. The sisters are barely literate. We see this in their whiny letters to their mother, which are full of misspellings. Sir Peter uses words to get his way. He lies when he needs to, and he makes threats if he must.

Ella's whole story is set in motion by some poorly chosen words. The fairy Lucinda's thoughtless gifts have lasting consequences. Her words have great power, but she doesn't use them carefully. The results are disastrous; we see clearly that the wrong words can do harm. In *Ella Enchanted*, we see that *how* you say something can be just as important as *what* you say.

When Ella finally breaks the curse, she is fighting the words inside her. "Words rose in me, filled my mouth, pushed against my lips. . . . I swallowed, forcing them down, but they tore at my throat," she tells the reader. Ella knows that the words she uses at this moment will change her life forever. If she speaks the wrong words at the wrong time, obedience will have won. Her own words ("Say yes and be happy. Say yes and live. Obey.") are a threat. But they also help her to assert her newfound power: "No! I won't marry you! I won't do it. No one can force me!" She calls out into the night, telling anyone who can hear that she won't marry Char. And once she is free of the curse, she knows that it is safe for her to say what she wants to say, because she is speaking from her own heart and mind.

Humor

Throughout *Ella Enchanted*, Ella finds humor in many situations. Like many people, Ella uses humor as a way to cope with challenges. She rebels against Mandy's orders with teasing and silliness. For relief, she clowns around and does imitations. And she can joke about a bad experience.

When she is taken prisoner by the ogres she manages to make *them* laugh, even though they plan to eat her.

> I offered to share [my food] with them, but my only answer was a collective shudder.
>
> "You might enjoy it," I said. "Perhaps you'd find that you prefer broccoli to flesh and legumes to legs."
>
> The last suggestion made them laugh.
>
> The youngest ogre told SEEf in Ogrese, "Maybe we should get to know our meals better. This one makes jokes."

As a narrator, Ella often uses her wit to amuse herself and the readers of her story. Humor isn't just a tool for her; it is an important part of her character. We see this throughout the book.

Ella uses humor in her descriptions of a scene. For example, she attempts to identify the fairies at the wedding by their small feet: "Ordinary foot. Small, but not small enough. Ordinary. Ordinary. Ordinary. Very tiny! Very tiny!"

Ella also uses humor in her interactions with other characters, whether or not the others are aware of it. The jokes she makes at her stepsisters' expense go unnoticed by them, but not by the reader. Ella can make jokes at her own expense, too. She describes her attempts to sing notes in music class, although she cannot carry a tune and a classmate covers her ears. At last she thinks she can sing, but everyone around her thinks differently:

> I hit the note. She played another. I sang it. She played a scale. I sang every note. I beamed. I'd always wished I could sing. I sang the scale again, louder. Perfect!

> "That's enough, young lady. You must sing when I tell you to, and not otherwise."

Ella seems to connect best with other characters who have a sense of humor, like her mother, Mandy, Areida and, of course, Char. From their first meeting, the reader can tell that humor is a key ingredient in Ella and Char's relationship. Laughter comes up in most scenes between them. Despite Ella's sadness on the day of her mother's funeral, Char can make her smile with his stories and his gentle teasing. She notices at that first meeting that his laugh isn't ridiculing but "a happy laugh at a good joke." Char also seems to know just what to say about her mother: that Lady Eleanor used to make him laugh.

In their correspondence, Ella and Char are witty, putting humor into their descriptions of their daily lives. The same sort of humor can be found in most of their conversations—they both make funny observations about the world around them, and they like to play with words. Humor is one of the things that bonds these two people. It is also one of Ella's most important qualities as a person and narrator. Her story would be very different without it.

Love

Ella and Char spend a lot of time thinking about what love means. Love, but not romance, because they have had very little time for romance in their courtship. But it seems to them that they have loved each other since the beginning. And love, they agree, "should not be dictated." They are two independent people.

Love is an important theme in *Ella Enchanted* because of the power it has to affect people's lives in important ways. Her mother's love helps Ella to grow up as strong and confident as it is possible for her to be while under the curse. Mandy may be able to do magic, but it is the strength of her love that helps Ella through difficult situations. Sir Peter may be intelligent and strong-willed, but he does not love his daughter. It is the *absence* of his love that affects Ella.

In the end, it is love that enables Ella to break the fairy's spell. She is able to break it on her own because, finally, she has sufficient reason. "I'd had to have reason enough, love enough to do it, to find the will and the strength," Ella tells the reader.

Up to this point, no event or person, however important, has been sufficient to end the curse. Ella's love for Mandy and her mother is great, but Ella was never in a position to do something so important for them that it would break the bonds of the fairy's curse.

Ella tells the reader: "My safety from the ogres hadn't been enough; zhulpH's rescue hadn't been enough . . . my slavery to Mum Olga hadn't been enough. Kyrria was enough. Char was enough." When she chooses to rescue Char by refusing him, she also rescues herself.

Once she realizes she is free, Ella can act on her great love for Char yet again—by turning around and proposing to him. Love is a driving force, and along with the gift of her independence, it is also Ella's happy ending.

Thinking about the themes

- Is there one theme in *Ella Enchanted* that is more important to you than the others? What makes it important?
- How do you use humor to deal with events in your own life?
- If Ella's story were narrated by another character—Mandy, for example—what themes do you think that narrator would emphasize?
- Is choosing to obey someone different from being forced to obey? How?

Ella Enchanted includes an enormous number of characters, both human and nonhuman. Here is a brief list of some of the major ones, followed by lengthier descriptions of the most important characters:

Ella of Frell	fifteen-year-old girl, narrator of the story
Sir Peter of Frell	Ella's father
Lady Eleanor	Ella's mother
Mandy	household cook (and Ella's fairy godmother)
Prince Charmont	son of King Jerrold, heir to the throne of Kyrria
Lucinda	fairy who gave Ella her "gift"
Dame Olga ("Mum Olga")	mother of Hattie and Olive, later Ella's stepmother
Hattie and Olive	Dame Olga's daughters
King Jerrold	king of Frell
Areida	Ella's best friend at school, an Ayorthaian
SEEf	ogre who "captures" Ella
Sir Stephan	one of Char's knights

Ella of Frell: The book's main character, Ella, is the fifteen-year-old daughter of Sir Peter and Lady Eleanor of Frell. A strong-willed, intelligent girl, she has been battling Lucinda's gift of obedience since birth. "Instead of making me docile, Lucinda's curse made a rebel of me," she tells the reader. "Or perhaps I was that way naturally."

Ella the rebel, the clumsy girl and bad dancer who describes herself as "skinny" and "spiky," looking like a grasshopper in a green dress, is an unusual fairy-tale heroine.

Raised by her mother and Mandy, the cook, Ella shares her mother's playfulness and sense of humor. As a young child she is ordered by Mandy to bring "more almonds" from the pantry. She returns with only two, following orders exactly "while still managing to frustrate the cook's true wishes." She and Mandy battle each other in this loving way, with Lady Eleanor laughing and egging them on.

"Once heard, always remembered is the way with languages and me," says Ella of her gift for words. At first, she mimics the parrots in the royal menagerie, but soon she is speaking Gnomic. She quickly learns how to communicate with different kinds of people and creatures, which helps her throughout her adventures. Her ability to listen and understand draws people (and elves) to her. It also allows her to tame a band of ogres, keeping them from turning her into dinner.

Ella of Frell is a complicated person, who is both loving and angry. Living with a fairy's curse takes its toll on her. She can be sarcastic and unkind. She bloodies the nose of a childhood friend who takes advantage of her. Ordered to pick up a dust ball, Ella grinds it into Hattie's face. More often she expresses her anger verbally, using her sharp wit to mock her tormentors. At one point, Ella tells Dame Olga that Hattie is "as clever as she is beautiful."

At the same time, Ella is brave, setting off alone on a journey into strange territory and fighting not just ogres but her own destiny. For Ella, the ultimate act of bravery—finding the strength and courage to break the curse—requires a battle with something invisible.

Ella's strength and independence continue to serve her well after her marriage to Char. Rather than taking a royal title, she becomes the Court Linguist and Cook's Helper. This complicated girl isn't your average princess.

Sir Peter of Frell: Ella's father is a clever and unethical businessman. When she was born, he was "away on a trading expedition, as usual," and he never learns about Lucinda's curse. As Mandy points out, he would just use her in his dishonest business dealings if he knew about it. The head maid thinks that on the inside, Sir Peter is just "ashes mixed with coins and a brain."

When we first meet Sir Peter, during his wife's funeral, he attempts to take his daughter's hand. Ella pulls away, and her father "never took my hand again." After the funeral, he presses the weeping Ella's face to his chest, but not to comfort her. He is "only trying to muffle my noise." He tells her to go away until she can be quiet.

Ella is uncomfortable with her father and doesn't trust him. Sir Peter tells her that he's selfish, impatient, and always gets his own way—and it's true. Also enterprising and strong-willed, he seems to appreciate those qualities in Ella. Yet he still seeks to control her. When he cannot manipulate her with gifts or flattery, he uses forceful commands. "The anger in his eyes was so tightly coiled that I didn't know what would happen if the spring were tripped," she says of her father.

He may call her brave, but Sir Peter doesn't treat Ella with respect. He is willing to force her to marry an old man in order to restore his fortunes. When Sir Peter leaves after his wedding, he doesn't seem to care what happens to Ella when she's left with Dame Olga. Although he states that she should not be treated as a servant, Sir Peter doesn't respond to Ella's letter when she tells him that's exactly what's happening to her.

Mandy: The cook is "bossy, giving orders almost as often as she drew breath." She has always been fiercely protective of Ella. After Lady Eleanor's death, Mandy seems to be the only person in Ella's world who is concerned about her well-being.

When Mandy reveals to Ella that she is her fairy godmother, Ella finds it hard to believe. "She couldn't be a fairy," Ella thinks. "Fairies were thin and young and beautiful... who ever heard of a fairy with frizzy gray hair and two chins?" Chins and all, Mandy really is a fairy.

Mandy gives Ella one of the most useful tools she could possibly have: a magic book, which ensures that Ella has the information she needs to cope with the difficulties of her time at school. When Ella is turned into a servant by her stepfamily, it is Mandy who steps in and takes her on as an assistant cook so that she can keep an eye on Ella and protect her.

Her strong character and her sense of right and wrong are clearly shown when Mandy explains to Ella the difference between big and small magic. Mandy will not do big magic because big magic has big—and possibly dangerous—consequences.

Overall, Mandy's manner is gruff and she is abrupt and bossy even with her goddaughter. However, she is a wise and loving character who will do anything, *except big magic*, for her beloved Ella.

Prince Charmont: Heir to the throne of Kyrria, Char is both Ella's true love and her best friend. He is two years older than Ella and has a royal bearing like his father's. Like the king, he has tawny curls and swarthy skin—with a sprinkling of freckles across his nose that Ella finds "surprising on such a dark face."

Char is open and playful, with a talent for making people feel at ease. The first time he and Ella meet, he begins by telling her something nice about her mother: that she made him laugh. Later, he compliments Ella by saying she's as funny as Lady Eleanor was. Laughter is a word that comes up often in connection with Char. No one else seems to be able to make Ella laugh; humor is important in their relationship. Even in the most difficult times, Ella and Char can find something to laugh about together. Plus, he's the only person apart from her mother who will slide down the banister with her!

Although Ella fears he will think her foolish for putting herself in danger just to attend the giants' wedding, Char actually admires her courage, saying to his knights, "If all the maids in Kyrria could tame ogres, we would have much less to do." While others want Ella to behave in certain ways, Char appreciates her need for freedom. He does have his flaws, though. He confesses to Ella that, while he is slow to anger, he is slow to forgive others.

Char is loyal to, and protective of, those he loves, but he is deeply hurt and angry when he thinks Ella has lied to him. "A thousand times a day I swear never to think of her." When Ella's identity is revealed at the third ball, however, he is overjoyed. Instead of being bitter or resentful, he is simply happy to be reunited with her.

Lucinda: Though we don't see much of her, Lucinda is one of the most important characters in the book; it is her action that sets Ella's story in motion. She "satisfies every cherished idea of a fairy," observes Ella when she sees Lucinda for the first time. Tall, graceful, and beautiful, Lucinda may look like an ideal fairy, but she uses her magic powers in less than ideal ways.

Lucinda's problem is that she is reckless; she doesn't stop to consider the consequences of her actions, and others must live with them. According to Mandy, Lucinda is a show-off who wants people to "thank her when she gives them one of her awful gifts."

In addition to the "gift" of obedience she gives Ella, we see how the consequences of her gifts affect other recipients, like the newlywed giants who will never be apart for even a minute.

Not until she has to spend time under some of her own spells does Lucinda understand what she's been doing to others. "What did I bring on those poor, innocent people?" She vows never to do big magic again, although this means she can't revoke Ella's gift. However, she does her best, using small magic, to help Ella find her way out of the situation.

Dame Olga ("Mum Olga"): Ella's stepmother has been called an "unpleasant conniver" by Sir Peter. When Ella first meets Dame Olga after Lady Eleanor's funeral, she finds herself "engulfed from behind by two chubby arms." Ella sees a "tall, plump lady with long and wavy honey-colored tresses" and a pasty white face "with twin spots of rouge on the cheeks."

A titled lady of Frell, Dame Olga marries Sir Peter for his money and discovers—too late—that he doesn't have any. But she is bound to him by Lucinda's "gift" of love, so she takes out her frustration and disappointment on her stepdaughter, Ella. Learning from Hattie about Ella's strange obedience, the previously "kittenish" Olga turns bossy and makes her stepdaughter into a servant. She is unkind to Ella from then on. Only when she sees Prince Charmont propose to her stepdaughter instead of Hattie or Olive does Dame Olga once again pretend to care for Ella.

Hattie and Olive: The spoiled daughters of Dame Olga, these are Ella's wicked stepsisters. She sees them as smaller versions of Dame Olga, "but without the rouge."

Hattie is about two years older than Ella. This girl has no regard for other people's feelings or privacy. In Ella's house for the first time, she insists on poking through the manor. She examines Lady Eleanor's gowns and speculates about how much things cost. At that first meeting, Hattie also brags about herself, saying she (Hattie) will live in the palace someday. Her prominent front teeth lead Ella to observe that she is "like a rabbit," but, because of her personality, "a fat one, the kind Mandy liked to slaughter for stew."

It is Hattie who figures out that Ella must obey direct orders, and she exploits this secret as often as possible. At school, she is clever enough to keep it a secret for her own benefit, and orders Ella around only in private. Hattie is secretly jealous of Ella, and her sense of power comes from bullying her "friend." Being in charge makes Hattie feel important.

Olive is about Ella's age. She is clueless, loud, and always saying the wrong thing at the wrong time. While not as cruel as her older sister, she is also not as clever. Olive sees what works for Hattie and tries to imitate her, with some success. Olive's main concerns seem to be money and food. She eventually marries an elderly man in exchange for a payment of twenty KJs a day and a white cake with every meal.

Thinking about the characters

- Does Ella share any of her father's characteristics, and if so, which ones?

- How would you describe Ella's personality? Do you see anything of yourself in her?

- The author uses physical descriptions to tell us something about certain characters' personalities. What are some of the other ways in which Gail Carson Levine reveals Ella's character to us?

How have people reacted to Gail Carson Levine's take on Cinderella? They've been enchanted—the response to *Ella Enchanted* has been overwhelmingly positive. In 1998, *Ella Enchanted* was voted a Newbery Honor Book by a committee representing the children's librarians of the American Library Association (ALA). You may see the silver medal on the book's cover. The Newbery selection committee called *Ella Enchanted* "an outstanding debut by talented newcomer Levine. She has . . . deepened our appreciation of the original tale." The ALA also chose *Ella Enchanted* as one of 1998's Best Books for Young Adults and one of their Quick Picks for Young Adults.

Other people seem to agree. A reviewer from *School Library Journal* also felt Levine had deepened and enriched the original Cinderella story. The journal chose the book as one of its Best Books of 1997. *Publishers Weekly* did the same.

The *ALAN* (Assembly for Literature for Adolescents of the National Council of Teachers of English) *Review* also praised the author: "In a delightful and enchanting way, Levine has created a new lived-through experience with a well-known fairy tale." *Booklist* called the book "superbly plotted."

In an Amazon.com review of *Ella Enchanted*, Emilie Coulter notes that "Gail Carson Levine's examination of traditional female roles in fairy tales takes some satisfying twists and deviations from the original." She calls it "the most remarkable, delightful, and profound version of Cinderella you've ever read."

The fairy-tale elements of the book seem to appeal to everyone who reads it, and the character of Ella is someone whom readers find especially appealing. The *Horn Book* described her as a heroine who "discovers her inner strength by combating her greatest weakness." Readers admire Ella's spirit and independence.

Ella isn't just a book that adults think you should read—kids are excited about it, too. On a Web site where readers can post reviews, kids call it "awesome," "creative," and "excellent." In 1999, students from schools all over Vermont voted to give Gail Carson Levine the Dorothy Canfield Fisher Children's Book Award. The sponsoring committee believes *Ella Enchanted* "has all the marks of a classic in the making."

Thinking about what other people think of *Ella Enchanted*

- What do you think it means when a reviewer describes a book as a "lived-through" experience?
- Would you give *Ella Enchanted* an award? If so, why?

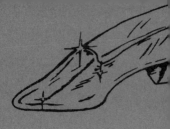

Glossary

Below you will find a list of words used in *Ella Enchanted*. The words may be new to you, or used in an unfamiliar way. Knowing what they mean will help you better understand the novel.

artifice insincere, phony, or false behavior

centaur a mythological creature that is half man, half horse

chicanery trickery or deception

felicitous well-suited to a person or situation; delightful or happy

fortitude inner strength

garrulous talking too much; given to rambling, boring speech

gavotte a sixteenth-century French dance. At the end of the dance, the couple was expected to kiss everyone in the room!

gryphon a mythical creature with the head and wings of an eagle and the hind legs and tail of a lion. Often spelled *griffin*.

hapless unfortunate; unlucky

harpy a mythological creature, half woman and half bird, usually bad-tempered and abusive

hart a male of the red deer species; a stag

hoodwink to deceive someone

hydra a mythological swamp creature with many heads

marchpane the sweet we know as marzipan, a paste made of almonds and sugar

minx a bold, pert, or impudent girl who doesn't behave as she is expected to. Often, but not always, used with affection.

proximity closeness

recto the right-hand page of an open book (see **verso**)

siren a part-human woman who bewitches listeners with her irresistible singing. According to some myths, sirens lure sailors to their deaths by causing them to sail their ships into rocks.

swain male admirer; a beau or suitor

topiary bushes, trees, and shrubs that are trimmed and pruned to resemble animal, human, or decorative shapes

unwavering constant; never-changing

verso the left-hand page of an open book (see **recto**)

voluminous full, taking up lots of space; having many folds

"... I just write a story. Self-discovery is one of the most wonderful things about writing, and you can't do that if you are too hard on yourself."

—Gail Carson Levine, *Authors & Artists for Young Adults*

"**I** write to the reader I was when I was a kid," said Gail Carson Levine in an interview with the *Christian Science Monitor*. So it shouldn't be surprising that she loved fairy tales as a child. Stories like "Ali Baba and the Forty Thieves" and "Beauty and the Beast" were among her favorites. She wants her own books to be "exciting and hard to put down. And I especially want them to be fun."

The critical inner voice (the "self-critic") that made painting an unhappy experience for Levine is very quiet when she writes, she has said. This doesn't mean that writing is always an easy or happy process. Some days, or some projects, are easier than others. Still, she loves being an author. "I love having written. Sometimes I love writing. I love to revise. Revising is my favorite part of writing," she told the *Christian Science Monitor*.

During the first nine years of her writing life, when every story she submitted was rejected, she learned from those rejections. She learned about revising her work, and she learned the importance of sticking with a story and trying to finish it, even if the writing is difficult. She advises young writers, "Suspend judgment of your work and keep writing . . . and be patient. Writing and glaciers advance at the same pace!"

When asked if she thinks bravery is a part of writing, Levine said, "Any creative act is scary and requires courage. You feel like you have only yourself to draw on, and what if you come up empty? But each creative act gives you a reserve of skill and experience."

Most of Levine's published work involves fairy-tale themes, and the stories take place in invented worlds. Is it hard to create a world from scratch instead of using the real world in your work? She talked about this in her *Christian Science Monitor* interview: "Making up one's own world is complicated. You have to keep track of it; you have to make sure that you are clueing the reader in. But working in [writing about] the real world is very hard, for me anyway. For other people it's not."

Levine discovers things about herself through writing, "but the discoveries aren't necessarily tied in with developing my characters," she has said. "It's messier than that. For example, after I wrote *Ella* I realized how hard it is for me to say no—how obedient I tend to be. But I wasn't aware of this during the writing."

When Gail Carson Levine begins a book, she doesn't always know the ending. While writing *Ella*, for example, she didn't know what cause or motivation would be sufficient to drive Ella to break the curse—she thought it might happen through her relationship with Hattie. As it turned out, the motivation was something (and someone) else.

Writers often experiment with ideas or themes that have attracted them in other books. For example, one reason for the many languages spoken in *Ella Enchanted* is Levine's admiration for *The Lord of the Rings*. Because she loved the way J. R. R. Tolkien created and used languages in the Rings trilogy, she wanted to try something similar in her book. Once she got started, she worked hard to make each of the languages spoken in *Ella Enchanted* very different.

Even after *Ella Enchanted* was published, Levine continued to take the writing class that had gotten her started. She also participated in groups with other writers. Today, she gives writing workshops at a middle school near her home. "I love it. . . . It's the best thing I do," she has said.

Gail Levine helps her middle-school writing students by encouraging them to explore new ideas. She talks a lot about that little voice in a writer's head, the "self-critic," and says "That voice is the enemy of creativity. Get that voice to shut up."

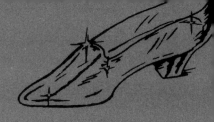

- **What does it feel like?:** What does it feel like to wake up from a hundred-year sleep? to have a magic cloak? to be turned into a bear? Gail Carson Levine says she likes to slow fairy tales down and help the reader experience extraordinary events like these. Think about a magic event in a favorite fairy tale, and imagine it happening to you. Write a short story, in the first person, about how it happens and what it feels like. You don't have to follow the plot of that fairy tale if you don't want to. Just take the event and place yourself in that moment. Then what happens?

- **The real story:** Levine wrote her own version of the Cinderella story to explain why the heroine behaves the way she does. She even included a simple explanation for something that happens in the story of the elves and the shoemaker. Is there a fairy tale or folk tale that has never quite made sense to you? Is there a character whose behavior is annoying or inexplicable? Tell the real story. Explain it to us. It doesn't have to be a novel (unless you want it to be); a short story will do.

- **Begin a fictional correspondence:** Letters are an important element in *Ella Enchanted*. Ella (and the reader) learn a lot from the letters that appear in Mandy's magic book. Ella's correspondence with Char is how the two friends grow even closer, sharing their lives and their ideas with each other. "It is great good luck that I have a pen and paper and a friend," Ella writes to Char. With an old or new friend, start a fictional correspondence. Each person creates a character, and the two of you write to each other as your characters for a period of time (weeks or months). You can start out knowing who each other's character is, or you can reveal him or her in your letters. Tell each other who you are, how you live, what interests you. Describe any adventures you have. Would your fictional selves use e-mail or pencil and paper? Would they include drawings or photos, or not? Be sure to copy all the letters so each person has a complete set. You can save them in a portfolio, share them with others, or keep them a secret.

• **Magic book:** If you could give Ella a piece of advice, or simply be the voice of a supportive friend, at any point during the story, what would you tell her? Write a letter that would appear in her magic book just when she needs it.

• **(Dis)obedience:** Ella was under a curse, and sometimes you may be unhappy about having to obey rules in so many areas of your life. Write about what tomorrow would be like if you woke up with total control over your life for the day. Or, write about how you would behave if Lucinda ordered you to be happy about obeying everyone's rules. In each case, think about a few things: Would you tell anyone, or would you try to keep your obedience (or disobedience) a secret? Why? How would your friends and family react to your new attitude?

Activities

- **Make a bestiary:** In medieval Europe, a bestiary was a beautifully illustrated book or manuscript that presents a collection of real and mythical animals. Make a bestiary of the creatures found in the royal menagerie in Frell, and add any other mythical animals that appeal to you. Along with your illustrations, include short descriptions of the creatures and anything interesting you know about them: their natural habitats, what (or whom) they eat, whether or not they're dangerous, and so on. Check your local library for information on medieval manuscripts—you might be able to find a reproduction of an original bestiary, or even the real thing.

- **Learn a language:** Though Ella's remarkable "once heard, always remembered" technique is *not* the way most of us learn languages, new languages are worth the effort. Begin to learn a second language. You can sign up for a class or find a friend or tutor to help you. There are also books, audiotapes, and Web sites available for people who are trying to learn languages on their own. If you're already bilingual, go for a third, or teach a language! Be a friend and tutor someone who wants to learn.

- **Give a gift:** Think about someone who's special to you. If you were that person's fairy godmother and could give him or her a magic gift, what would it be, and why? What would the consequences be? Once you've figured out what the best gift would be, write a card or letter to the recipient explaining what you wish for them. You can do this for a special occasion, like a birthday or wedding, or just because you feel like it. Gifts are always welcome—unless they're from Lucinda.

• **Meet the Japanese Cinderella:** It seems as though almost every culture or country you can think of has some version of the Cinderella story in its folklore. Chilean, Russian, Indian, Mexican, Himalayan, Japanese, Egyptian, and Chinese Cinderellas are just a few of the stories you'll find. Explore your local library or bookstore, and read as many as you can! You can ask a librarian for assistance. Notice how the stories differ from culture to culture and also how certain elements of the stories are the same all over the world. This is true of many other familiar fairy tales, so if you enjoy reading them, you can keep on reading around the world.

• **Start a writing group:** Many writers find it helpful to be part of a group or workshop in which they can share their work with other writers and exchange ideas about writing. They might do writing exercises together, like Gail Levine and her students. If this appeals to you, start a writing group! Invite a few interested friends or classmates to join. You may want to start with a fairly small group of four or five people. Find a regular meeting time (every few weeks, for example) and a meeting place. Perhaps you can get permission to meet at school. Decide whether one person will "lead" the group or that you'll take turns. Should members read one another's work before they meet? Be sure you have a way of getting copies to everyone. Then, set some ground rules. (For example, members need to be supportive and respectful of one another.) And begin your writing adventure!

• **Enjoy a cream trifle:** One of the dishes served at Sir Peter's manor is cream trifle. Trifle is a delicious dessert usually made with cream, fruit, and cake. It has been made for hundreds of years in many parts of the world. There are probably hundreds of different varieties. Here is an easy, no-cook version that you and your friends can make to serve at your own banquet.

Ingredients

1 16-ounce prepared pound cake
1 large jar of jam (strawberry, raspberry, blackberry)
A handful of fresh berries (strawberries, blackberries, raspberries, blueberries) for decoration
1 pint of whipping cream
1 small package of chopped walnuts (optional)

Directions

1. Wash your hands.
2. Mash up the cake, using a fork or your clean hands.
3. Pour the cream into a large mixing bowl. Using a whisk or an electric mixer, whip the cream. Ask an adult for help. Whisk (or mix) the cream until it becomes thick.
4. Put a layer of crushed cake in the bottom of a large, clear bowl. Then put a layer of jelly on top of the cake. Then spoon a layer of whipped cream over the jelly. (You could add a layer of chopped nuts, too!)
5. Repeat step 4 until the bowl is full, then top your dessert with a fluffy layer of whipped cream. Decorate the cream with the fresh berries of your choice.
6. Refrigerate your trifle for at least two hours before serving (cover the dish carefully with plastic wrap). Refrigerate any leftovers—they should be good for two or three days.

Other novels by Gail Carson Levine

Dave at Night (1999)

The Two Princesses of Bamarre (2001)

The Wish (2000)

The Princess Tales series:

   Cinderellis and the Glass Hill (2000)

   The Fairy's Mistake (1999)

   The Fairy's Return (2002)

   For Biddle's Sake (2002)

   Princess Sonora and the Long Sleep (1999)

   The Princess Test (1999)

Novels inspired by fairy tales

Beauty by Robin McKinley

The Forestwife by Theresa Tomlinson

Goose Chase by Patrice Kindl

The King's Equal by Katherine Paterson

Once upon a Marigold by Jean Ferris

Zel by Donna DiNapoli

Fairy tales

The Complete Brothers Grimm Fairy Tales edited by Lily Owens

The Complete Fairy Tales of Charles Perrault translated by Neil
   Philip

Bibliography

Books and interviews

Jones, J. Sydney. "Gail Carson Levine," *Authors & Artists for Young Adults.* Volume 37. Farmington Hills, Michigan: Gale Research, 2001.

Levine, Gail Carson. *Ella Enchanted.* New York: HarperCollins, 1997.

_____. *The Two Princesses of Bamarre.* New York: HarperCollins, 2001.

_____. *The Wish.* New York: HarperCollins, 2002.

_____. Interviews conducted via e-mail (November/December 2002) and phone (December 12, 2002).

Peacock, Scott, ed. *Contemporary Authors: A Bio-bibliographical Guide to Current Writers in Fiction, General Nonfiction, Poetry, Journalism, Drama, Motion Pictures, Television, and Other Fields.* Volume 166, pp. 205–206.

Newspapers and magazines

Bush, Elizabeth. Review of *Ella Enchanted, Bulletin of the Center for Children's Books,* Volume 50, May 1997, p. 327.

Cooper, Ilene. Review of *Ella Enchanted, Booklist,* April 15, 1997, p. 1423.

Deifendeifer, Anne. Review of *Ella Enchanted, Horn Book,* May–June 1997, p. 325.

Devereaux, Elizabeth and Diane Roback. Review of *Ella Enchanted, Publishers Weekly,* March 31, 1997, p. 75.

Kirkus Reviews. Review of *Ella Enchanted*, February 1, 1997, p. 225.

Metzger, Lois. "On Their Own," *New York Times Book Review*, November 21, 1999, p. 32.

Smith, Alice Case. Review of *Ella Enchanted*, *School Library Journal*, April 1997, p. 138.

Zipp, Yvonne. "The Fairy Tales of Now," *Christian Science Monitor*, January 11, 2001, p. 18.

Web sites

ALAN Review (Fall 1997):
http://scholar.lib.vt.edu/ejournals/ALAN/fall97/clipandfile.html

Review of *Ella Enchanted* and author biographical information:
www.alexlibris.com

Author information at HarperChildrens.com:
www.harperchildrens.com/hch/author/author/levine/

Gail Levine's biographical sketch written for the Eighth Book of Junior Authors and Illustrators, available through the Educational Paperback Association:
www.edupaperback.org/authorbios/Levine_GailCarson.html

Dorothy Canfield Fisher Award for *Ella Enchanted*:
www.mps.k12.vt.us/msms/dcf/ella.html

Ella Enchanted (A Book Report Page):
www.expage.com/ellaenchanted

The Cinderella Project:
www.usm.edu/english/fairytales/cinderella/cinderella.html